Go For It!

**Start Smart,
Have Fun &
Stay Inspired in
Any Activity**

by Patti Kelley Criswell
illustrated by Shannon Laskey

W9-CAZ-528

★ American Girl®

Published by American Girl Publishing, Inc.

Copyright © 2008 by American Girl, LLC

All rights reserved. No part of this book may be used or reproduced in any manner whatsoever
without written permission except in the case of brief quotations embodied in critical articles and reviews.

Questions or comments? Call 1-800-845-0005,
visit our Web site at **americangirl.com**,
or write to Customer Service, American Girl,
8400 Fairway Place, Middleton, WI 53562-0497.

Printed in China

08 09 10 11 12 13 LEO 10 9 8 7 6 5 4 3 2

All American Girl marks are trademarks of American Girl, LLC.

Editorial Development: Carrie Anton

Art Direction and Design: Camela Decaire

Production: Jeannette Bailey, Judith Lary, Mindy Rappe, Gretchen Krause

Illustrations: Shannon Laskey

Photography: istock, Getty Images, Fotosearch

Special thanks to: The Kalamazoo Figure Skating Club

All the instructions in this book have been tested. Results from testing were incorporated into this book.
Nonetheless, all recommendations and suggestions are made without any guarantees on the part of
American Girl Publishing, Inc. Because of differing tools, ingredients, conditions, and individual skills,
the publisher disclaims liability for any injuries, losses, or other damages that may result from using the
information in this book.

Dear Reader,

Have you always dreamed of becoming an ice-skater, a singer, or a violinist? Or what about a basketball star, an actress, or a drummer? Whatever your dreams are—even if you don't quite know what they are yet—it's time to make them come true by trying something new! It's time to *Go For It!*

Inside this book you'll learn how to conquer every challenge, from finding an activity that's right for you and trying out, to practicing and performing with confidence. We've included tips for talking with teammates and instructors, and, of course, lots of advice from girls just like you—athletes, artists, musicians, and more! They've shared the secrets of their success to help you stay balanced and be your personal best.

We've given you ideas for keeping your cool and for keeping it fun. Because that's really what it's all about—having a great time while feeling great, too!

Your friends at American Girl

ICE-SKATING CLASS
TUESDAYS
4-5 PM

Don't Miss the Volleyball Tournament!
THIS SATURDAY AT NOON

Tennis Anyone?
SESSION ONE:
M, W, F
3-4:30
SESSION TWO:
T, Th, S
4-5:30
CALL COACH WILLIS!

School Play Tryouts!
THIS MONDAY
5:00 PM IN GYMNASIUM!

SWIM TEAM
SIGN-UPS
MONDAY
4 PM
NORTH POOL

Miss Harriette's Piano Lessons
LEARN TO PLAY THE MISS HARRIETTE WAY!
CALL TODAY! CALL TODAY! CALL TODAY! CALL TODAY! CALL TODAY! CALL TODAY! CALL TODAY! CALL TODAY!

ACE ACTING STUDIO
Beginners Welcome!

Give It a Try

Find an activity that's right for you!

Soul Skater

My first memory of wanting to be a skater was when I was two years old. I loved watching the way ice-skaters on TV moved. They seemed to have the ability to "fly" across the ice. But because I had a problem with the bone in my arm, my parents said, "No, it's too dangerous. How about dance instead?"

I tried taking dance lessons. It was O.K., but it just wasn't skating. I took dance for about five years, and toward the end, I found every excuse not to go. I remember that there were girls at my studio who **loved** dancing. I was so jealous of them.

When I finally couldn't take it anymore, I sat down with my parents and asked them what needed to happen for me to become an ice-skater. They talked to my doctor, who said that when I reached ten years old, I'd be clear to skate. So I waited patiently for my tenth birthday, and the first time I stepped onto the ice, I was so excited that I was shaking.

Now I've been skating for three years and have loved every minute. I've worked hard to be able to be the skater who jumps, spins, and "flies" on the ice. It hasn't always been easy, though. Skating is hard work! My parents have been very supportive and realize that skating is my passion. I think it will always be a big part of who I am.

Sometimes people ask me why I picked skating. I don't know for sure, but I do know that I feel the most like the real, true me when I'm on the ice. I look forward to skating more than anything else I do. I can honestly say that every time I step onto the ice, my heart still skips a beat.

—An American girl

6

What's Right for You?

You're trying to find an activity that is just right for you—something that makes you feel great inside. Maybe it's music, dance, acting, or sports. But with so many options, how do you choose? Try our game to help you find your way!

START
(fill in the blank)
looks like fun.
Do you know people who do this activity?
NO
Ask around for people who do. Then return to Start.
YES
Ask Questions
Do you need to practice when you're at home, too? If so, how often?
What kind of equipment do you need?
Where do you get the equipment?
Where do you practice and perform?
What do you like about this activity?
What do you dislike about the activity?
Still interested?
No
RETURN TO START
Yes!
TURN TO NEXT PAGE

Do you have **equipment?**

NO

Can you get equipment easily?

YES

NO

Talk to your parents for **ideas.** If you can't get equipment, you may have to consider an activity that is a better fit.

Return to Start.

YES!

Congratulations!

You're ready to try something new. It's exciting, and maybe even a little scary. But don't worry! Sometimes you just have to take a risk, keep an open mind, and **jump right in!**

Tryout Time

Sometimes you have to try out or audition to be part of an activity. This is your chance to show your talent AND your personality. Remember, you can only do your best, so take a deep breath and give it your all.

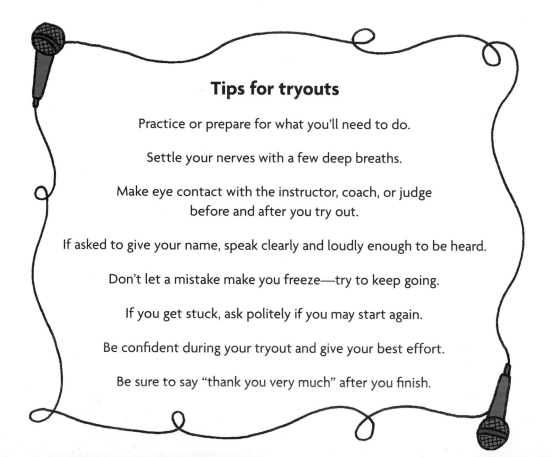

Tips for tryouts

Practice or prepare for what you'll need to do.

Settle your nerves with a few deep breaths.

Make eye contact with the instructor, coach, or judge before and after you try out.

If asked to give your name, speak clearly and loudly enough to be heard.

Don't let a mistake make you freeze—try to keep going.

If you get stuck, ask politely if you may start again.

Be confident during your tryout and give your best effort.

Be sure to say "thank you very much" after you finish.

Good Start

You're about to try something you've never done before, meet new people, get instruction from a new adult, and lots of other firsts. It's normal to be feeling all kinds of emotions, but don't worry! When excitement gets the best of you, use the hints below to help you out.

Jumping Bean

You just can't wait to get started! In fact, you are about to burst with excitement. Just make sure your enthusiasm doesn't get in the way of learning and listening.

Hint: Don't hide your spirit, but do show your instructor that you know when to settle in and pay attention.

Shy Girl

You're feeling shy—and that's O.K.—but don't let your shyness be mistaken for a bad attitude. Your body language matters, so be sure that you look as if you want to be there, even if it takes extra time to warm up to new things.

Hint: Eye contact and nodding your head let others know that you're listening.

Show-Off

Even if you've read all about this activity and know everything there is to know, that doesn't mean you have to show your stuff all on the first day. There will be plenty of time to show what you know—and probably learn a lot, too!

Hint: Ask other people questions about themselves instead.

Fresh Face

If you're joining an established group, you might feel like the odd girl out. But take heart! It might take some time, but a new face may be exactly what's needed to give the group a boost.

Hint: Hold your head up high and be confident. If you are friendly and willing to learn, you'll fit right in in no time.

Miss Cranky

Maybe you're having a bad day or you've been overdoing it lately. Either way, you're tired, you're moody, and you'd rather be home in bed. It's no fun feeling stressed, but you don't want to bring down everyone around you, too.

Hint: Make a choice to shake off the grouchies or step out for the day. Nothing can be gained by having a bad attitude—and it's not fair to others.

17

Practice Pointers

It doesn't matter if you're learning piano, Ping-Pong, or a part in a play—practicing is the only way to get better.

Make it a routine
Save time each week to practice. The more you stick to this schedule, the easier it will be to fit practice into your weekly routine.

Warm up
Athletes stretch their muscles, musicians warm up their fingers, and singers tune their voices. Ease into practice with gentle exercises to get your mind and body in the zone.

What do you know?
Start with what you do well to gain confidence, and pump yourself up to work on more challenging things later.

Drill a skill
Pick one skill that you want to get better at, and do it over and over—and over again! You'll train your brain and, before you know it, the skill will seem super simple.

End strong
Create a traditional way to end each practice, such as writing down your progress or high-fiving your teammates. The point is to finish on a high note.

Big

Important Point

Does practice make perfect? Nah. Nobody is perfect all the time—not even the pros. But practicing will make you better; it just will.

Time to Shine

You've spent hours practicing and rehearsing. All that's left is to show the world what's come of your hard work. As you get ready to play or perform, follow the tips in this timeline to be your best for the big day.

Plan
Lay out what you plan to wear and anything you need to bring along. And most importantly, get a good night's sleep!

Eat
Eat a good breakfast. You'll want plenty of energy to see you through your day.

Double-Check
Do you have everything you need?

BRING!

Butterflies and Jitters
No matter what you call it, feeling nervous before a performance or game is perfectly normal. To help calm down, repeat a positive phrase, such as "I can do this," "I know what to do," or "I'm ready."

I can do this!

Breathe

To calm down, breathe in slowly,
hold it for a few seconds, and
then breathe out slowly.

Focus

When it's time to perform, your body may
feel stronger and more excited than usual.
Just go with it and know that you have
the ability to be amazing. If you do make
a mistake, keep going and look confident.
The audience may not even notice.

Think Positive

Keep your thoughts positive. It's a proven fact that good things can come from positive thinking. If you see yourself as a star, you'll shine like one!

Girl Advice

Need to calm your nerves? Try these tips from girls!

I pretend that I'm a world-famous athlete and that this is one more game. It works! —Anna, age 12, volleyball player

Before I perform, I do a lot of stretching and take deep breaths. —Jenna, age 10, ice-skater

I just tell myself that I can do it, and the nervousness melts away. —Madeline, age 10, basketball player

I tell my friends when I'm nervous, and they tell me jokes to help calm me down.
—Alisha, age 12, ice-skater

I get all my stuff organized ahead of time. It helps because I don't have to worry about forgetting something.
—Emily, age 8, cellist

I think of how good I am going to feel after I perform. I also keep my eye on my teacher at first. After a few minutes, I settle in and don't feel so nervous.
—Laura, age 8, violinist

I practice my lines so many times that I don't have to worry about whether I know them. That way I can focus on my acting. I also don't look at the audience until I am done!
—Natalie, age 11, actor

Calling It Quits

Dear American Girl,

I can't stand taking piano lessons! I've tried talking to my mom but I can't convince her. Even when I learned a whole song, I didn't enjoy it. I want to, but inside I just don't.

—Sour Notes

Not everything that sounds like fun is going to be. You tried it, and it didn't work out. Talk to your parents and help them understand why you want to quit. They want you to find what's right for you but also want to make sure you've given the piano a fair chance. If you've given your all and just don't like it, ask their advice on what to do. If you do quit, use this experience to choose something different.

Big

Important Point

You're not going to love (or succeed at) everything you try—and you shouldn't be expected to. Every experience you have is valuable because it helps you get to know yourself just a little bit better.

Dear American Girl,

I tried out for the school play and didn't make it. I've always loved acting, so I was really upset. Now I'm scared to try new things. What if I fail again or am not good at anything?

—Drama Queen in Training

You set your sights on something that didn't work—but it was only one audition! Everyone is good at something; you just need to find where your light shines. You may need to try lots of activities (including trying out for the next play) before you find what's right for you. Don't give up, and try, try again!

Dear American Girl,

I was talked into playing an instrument that I knew in my heart I didn't want to play. I felt forced, but now I want to quit. I'm afraid of disappointing my teacher, and I know my band friends will make it a big deal, too. I feel embarrassed every time I play, but I feel trapped. What should I do?

—Band Bummed

Remember the voice inside you that said, "I really don't want to do this"? It's there for a reason. Listen to yourself and talk to your parents and teacher about how you feel. Be fair to your fellow band members (especially if you have a concert coming up), and to yourself. Ending your music career may be the right choice. Whatever you decide, chalk this one up to experience and find something that you're actually excited to try.

27

Going for Great!

Find your groove in your new activity.

Focused on Fun

When I was younger I wanted to try everything, and my parents were very supportive. I tried all sorts of activities hoping to find something that was just right for me. Everything sounded like so much fun, so I tried swimming, softball, horseback riding, dance, and Tae Kwan Do.

Then, because I started to have trouble in school, I had to cut down on my extra activities for a while. It turned out that I needed glasses, and with some extra tutoring, I caught up quickly, but my confidence was low. I missed being active and part of something.

I hadn't been to Tae Kwon Do in a while, but I decided to re-join. I was scared that I had forgotten everything, but I built up my bravery and stepped back on the mats. This time, though, it felt different. Instead of having Tae Kwon Do being just one more thing to try, I found that having time to focus made it even more fun. My instructor helped me see that

Tae Kwon Do could also be rewarding. He had me imagine all the worries of the day being left behind as I stretched. My stress disappeared as I broke boards with my hands and feet. I started to feel fit, strong, and powerful again. It felt great!

Off the mats, things started to turn around for me, too. My focus at school kept improving, and I had a much brighter mood. I even made some new friends.

Day by day, my confidence grew, and I soon set new goals for myself. I earned a new belt color and even went to a tournament. When I placed in the competition, I couldn't stop smiling. Next year I want to go to the state tournament and, one day, earn a black belt. Even though it has been a lot of hard work, I'm happier than ever!

—An American girl

31

Leading the Way

Make the most of your coach or instructor by following these leads.

Work together
Ask your instructor what he or she expects from you, and discuss the goals you'd like to reach.

Clock's ticking
Be on time and ready with everything you need to learn.

Don't take it personally

Remember that criticism is how you learn, grow, and get better. Let your instructor know that you hear and understand him or her.

Make it fun

A great attitude makes everything more fun. So be positive and let your spirit shine.

Big Important Point

There is nothing worse than giving your all and going unnoticed. But knowing on the inside that you did your best is really the greatest reward. It would be great if your instructor could also be your biggest fan, but that doesn't always happen. Make sure that you are doing your best and feeling proud of it.

Grown-Up Gab

The relationship between you and your instructor or coach is an important one. So what do you do if a problem comes up? Talking to instructors can be intimidating, but honestly, they can't help you if they don't know what's going on. Ask a parent to help you practice with our conversation starters. When you're ready, approach your instructor with confidence.

Conversation starters

Get his or her full attention:

"Hey, coach, when you have a few minutes, can we talk?"

Show that you value his or her opinion:

"Miss Sarah? I've been having some trouble lately and I was wondering if I could get your advice."

Ask for one-on-one time:

"Remember the other night at practice? It's really been bothering me. Do you think we could talk about what happened?"

"I'm not sure what you meant. Could you explain it in a different way?"

Get more direction:

Say thanks and ask for more:

"Hi, Mrs. H. I really appreciate the extra help lately. Do you think we could talk more about the feedback you gave me last week?"

Remember to stay cool, calm, and respectful when talking with your instructor. If after talking you are still frustrated, talk with your parent to come up with a new plan.

Team Talk

"She doesn't pass the ball!"

"She totally missed that one!"

Use pick-me-ups, not put-downs. Work hard to notice what others are doing *right*, not what they're doing wrong.

If you're frustrated, don't take it out on some-one else. Talk with your instructor privately, vent to a parent, or write your thoughts in a journal. Just leave others out of it.

Working with a group of people isn't always easy. If you find yourself using put-downs and gossip against someone else, you're only hurting your group. STOP. You need to work together without bringing the whole group down.

"She always forgets her lines!"

"She's hogging the music stand."

Trust that everyone is doing the best he or she can. His or her best may not look like your best. It may change from day to day.

Working as a team means talking through problems. Nicely bring up the issue and work together to resolve it.

Oops!

Nobody's perfect. Even the most talented professionals make mistakes, and you will, too! It's O.K. Just take it easy on yourself and try to bounce back quickly. If you do, you'll show a spirit others will respect and admire.

Five things you should know about mistakes

1. They happen to everyone.

2. Don't let them slow you down.

3. Most people in the audience don't even notice when one is made—really!

4. They help you know what you need to work on.

5. Once you learn from them, they're no longer mistakes; they're lessons learned.

Shake it off

When friends and teammates make mistakes, help them through the experience. Create a team tradition for dealing with "oops" moments. For example, if a girl gets down on herself for making a mistake, act as a team and shake your arms on the sidelines to signal "Shake it off."

Attitude Check

When competition doesn't go your way, do you find it hard to handle? Keep track of your choices below to see how well you carry yourself when you compete.

1. You just lost a close basketball game. As you walk off the court, your teammate loudly says, "If the referee had been watching, we'd have won!" You respond:

   a. "We'll do better next time."
   b. "Hey, ref! Time to get new glasses!"

2. You sign up for the school chess team. When you tell your friend about it, she does the same. You . . .

   a. look forward to having someone to play against for practice.
   b. tell her to stop copying you, because chess is *your* thing.

3. Your synchronized skating team is doing great until your teammate falls. You tell her . . .

   a. "It's O.K., mistakes happen," and comfort her the best you can.
   b. that she ruined the team's chances of winning.

40

4. You spend hours practicing your flute and try harder than anyone else. Your friend barely picks up her flute, but she was given a higher position in the band than you! When the announcement is made, you . . .

    a. take a deep breath, and then congratulate your friend.
    b. make a scene by angrily storming out of the room.

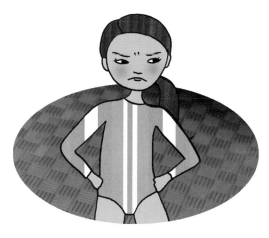

5. You think your gymnastics coach favors the other girls, spending more time with them and praising every little thing they do. You . . .

    a. talk to your coach about how you feel.
    b. demand that your parents find you a new gym.

6. You've had the lead in almost every school performance. But when the cast list is posted for the new musical, your name is not listed for a speaking part. You:

    a. talk to the drama club teacher about helping out backstage.
    b. make jokes about those who did get leads. After all, they didn't deserve them!

Answers

If you answered mostly "A"s, then you know that being a true winner has little to do with scoreboards, ribbons, or trophies. It's about attitude. If you answered mostly "B"s, use the tips below to put you back in the winner's circle.

1. A good sport respects referees' decisions, even if it means biting your tongue.

2. Hold on! You don't own the rights to any activity. Accept and welcome your friend—and anyone else—to your team.

3. Supporting your teammates is never optional. Remember, winning doesn't come before being kind.

4. It's disappointing not to get the position you want, but taking it out on a friend isn't the answer. Forget about where you sit and just focus on doing your best.

5. If you need more attention from coaches than you're getting, speak up. They can't help if they don't know what's going on.

6. Cutting others down only makes you look bad. Instead, learn as much as you can and help boost the spirit of the show.

Girl Advice

Here's what girls have to say about how they win and lose with grace.

I'm a no-pressure kind of person. When I get all stressed out about winning, I don't play as well. I just try to have fun.
—Amy, age 10, softball player

If I don't do well, but I've tried my hardest, I don't feel bad, because I know that I can't do any better than my best.
—Grace, age 9, dancer

I lose respect for people who make excuses when they lose. If you lose, you lose— chalk it up and move on.
—Brenna, age 11, gymnast

We slap hands with the opposing team before and after the game, and say "good game" no matter what the score. It makes me feel really good and proud to be part of my team.
—Morgan, age 13, volleyball player

I don't know anyone who doesn't want to win, but you have to keep it in perspective and remember that someone has to lose. I just try to do my best and have fun. That's all I can do.
—Anna, age 12, violinist

When you win, put off celebrating until you shake hands with the other person or team. It's the classy thing to do.
—Natalie, age 11, martial artist

Cool Competitor

Dear AG,

My friends and I entered our talent show at school just for fun, but the other people in the show are so serious—all they care about is winning! They keep talking about how they are going to beat us. If they win, they'll be bragging all year! We just want to have fun. What should we do?

—Just Want to Have Fun

Amer
840
Mi

Some people place too much importance on the prize instead of the process—which is learning about performing, doing your best, and, yes, having FUN. For now, focus on your part of the show and enjoy yourself along the way. The other contestants might win the talent show. If they do, congratulate them to set a good example. Being a good sport with a great attitude means more than winning any day.

Big
Important Point
A game well played is the real goal. Sure, winning is great, but it's short-lived—a winning attitude lasts. Competition makes us better. Without it, the thrill of victory wouldn't exist!

Dear American Girl,

I am in swing choir and keep getting solo parts. My friends keep getting angry at me because the choir teacher picks me. I feel guilty all the time. How can I make them stop?

—Sad Singer

Your "friends" are not being very friend-like right now. Being jealous of your success is understandable, but being angry and taking it out on you is not O.K. Try to ignore their comments and change the subject when it comes up. So long as you are not bragging about your solos, you have no reason to feel guilty. So sing your heart out!

Am
8400
Middlet

Dear American Girl,

I'm in dance four days a week. I love it, but the problem is that my mom is too competitive. She is always telling me to try harder—even when I feel I'm doing my best. She won't stop, and at times it's so bad that I want to quit something I really enjoy. What should I do?

—Miserable in Minnesota

Your mom probably just wants to be encouraging, even if her comments have the opposite effect. No one likes to feel that kind of pressure, especially when you are giving it your all. Have a heart-to-heart talk with your mom to explain how you feel. Most of the time parents want to be helpful, so be sure to let her know what is—and is not—helpful to you. If she does it again, remind her of the talk the two of you had together.

Am
840
Midd

47

Keeping It Fun

Stay inspired to keep doing what you enjoy.

Go-Go-Go Girl

My family and I live very busy lives, and we learned the hard way that for everyone to be happy, we need to work together.

During baseball season, my brother practiced several nights a week and played games on weekends. I had rehearsals for the spring musical at school, as well as music lessons, homework, and Girl Scout meetings. My parents both were very busy with their jobs, and that's when it happened: a messy house and a packed schedule led to stress overload! Bickering erupted into a storm of fighting filled with tears. Our family just wasn't working together.

My parents called a family meeting, and we all ranked what on our schedules was most important to each of us. It wasn't easy, but we made changes that helped us individually and as a team.

We came up with creative ways to help one another, including scheduling five minutes to tidy up rooms on Wednesdays. We developed a system to get uniforms washed, music practiced, and homework done. It's amazing what can be done through teamwork!

To make sure we spend enough time together, we always try to eat dinner together and make meals for the week on Sunday—my brother and I have even learned to cook! When we can't have dinner as a family, we try to eat breakfast together or play cards before bed. On Friday nights, we order pizza and watch movies, just for fun. I'm proud of my family. We each had to give up a few things, but we got our happiness back. And that's what is most important.

—An American girl

51

Schedule Secrets

When life gets busy, get organized!

Check in with Mom

Prepare for each week on Sunday by scheduling anything new, such as a dentist's appointment, a sleepover at a friend's house, or an upcoming study group.

Every week

Make a weekly schedule of things that don't usually change, such as school hours, lessons, and practice times. Don't forget to schedule time for homework.

Time to prepare

Schedule time the night before a lesson, a practice, or a game to prepare for the next day.

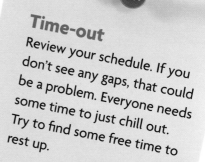

Time-out

Review your schedule. If you don't see any gaps, that could be a problem. Everyone needs some time to just chill out. Try to find some free time to rest up.

Clutter Control

If you've ever been late to practice because you couldn't find your knee pads or frantically looked for your flute music, then you know the importance of getting and *staying* organized. Clear the clutter and you'll cut the chaos, too!

Dump or donate

Toss the garbage, but donate items other people could use. Your space will be clean, and you'll feel better knowing you helped someone else.

Giveaway!

Easy schmeezy

Pack away what you don't use daily. Use smaller containers rather than one big bin (where items can get lost). Label each container for easy access to everything you need.

Get vertical

Use the height in your room to store items you like to look at but don't need to get to, such as trophies, pictures, and collectibles.

Pick—and pack up—papers

Keep school papers in your binder or backpack. Choose a binder, folder, or paper-sized box to store your best work.

Be predictable

If you have a uniform or equipment, always put it in the same bag, bin, or spot in your room so that you'll be able to find it fast.

On the Road

If you're back and forth between school and practice, the car could feel like your second home. Here are a few ways to make the most of a humdrum ride:

1. Keep a book or magazine in the car to read.

2. Take a "power nap." It'll make the trip fly by, and you'll be more rested when you arrive.

3. Leave a joke book in the car for when you need a good laugh.

4. Keep car copies of things you need to memorize, such as math facts, states and capitals, drama club lines, or Spanish vocabulary.

Car Kits

Organized auto bag

Keep the car clean and packed with necessities by filling a travel toiletries case with items you need on the road.

Just-in-case kit

Create a kit for your duffel bag of things you might need when you leave the house. Always forgetting your hair ties for the big game? Add them to your kit. You may also want to add a snack bar, a water bottle, sunscreen, and any other must-have items that are easily forgotten as you are running out the door.

In Too Deep?

Being your best means different things at different times. If you are tired and worn out, your "best" may look very different than if you're rested and ready to go. Put your best to the test and rate where you rank:

100%—Feeling great, so stay at that pace!

80%—Doing pretty well, but not completely at the top of your game. Take a look at what's slowing you down. Talk to your parents and make some changes fast.

50%—Losing steam and headed for burnout fast. Take a break and enjoy some down-time. Reconnect with family and friends. Sleep and eat well to get on the road to recovery.

25%—Heading nowhere! You may have bitten off more than you can chew. If you have a lot going on, it's time to lighten your schedule load!

Always tired?

Let's face it, you can't be at your best and be half asleep! To keep your energy level up all day, try to go to bed at the same time each night. If you have a hard time settling down, write your thoughts in a journal, listen to soothing music, or count backward from 100.

Part of feeling your best means being ready and alert, so it's important that you wake up feeling rested. If you're not getting enough ZZZs, you just may need to go to bed a little earlier. Before you know it, you'll be heading for dreamland and feeling better than ever.

Girl Advice

Try these tips about inspiration from girls like you!

When I need inspiration, I think of my team. I know they are counting on me to do my best, and I don't want to let them down.
—Abby, age 12, softball player

I like to go to concerts and watch the professionals play—they inspire me. Then, when I practice, I pretend I'm one of them!
—Natalie, age 11, violinist

I get inspired to work on my game so that I can beat my brothers!
—Madeline, age 10, basketball player

Memories of my grandma playing the piano inspired me to play. It makes her so happy to listen to me that I just want to keep on playing!
—Amy, age 10, pianist

Music inspires me. My friend and I always listen to the same song before our games—it's our good-luck song.
—Morgan, age 13, volleyball player

My goals are my inspiration. I set my sights on one thing I want to improve and focus on getting better.
—Brenna, age 11, gymnast

Now you know a bit more about how to practice with passion and perform with grace. You know how to solve problems, listen to your heart, and trust your instincts. Whatever you do for fun, go at it with all your soul. Take care of yourself along the way and above all, have fun and let your spirit soar. In other words—GO FOR IT!

Write to us!

Send your true *Go For It!* stories to:

Go For It Editor
American Girl
8400 Fairway Place
Middleton, WI 53562

(Photos can't be returned. All comments and suggestions received by American Girl Publishing may
be used without compensation or acknowledgment.)

Here are some other American Girl books you might like:

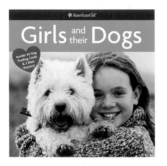

❑ I read it.

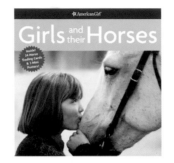

❑ I read it.

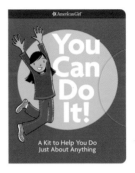

❑ I read it.

❑ I read it.

❑ I read it.

❑ I read it.

Perk-Up-
Your-Practice
Cards

Perk-Up-
Your-Practice
Cards

Perk-Up-
Your-Practice
Cards

Perk-Up-
Your-Practice
Cards

Quiz bowl

Ask your parent to give you the definitions of the terms and you try to identify them. For example: the setter in volleyball is the girl responsible for playing the ball on the second contact of each play.

© 2008 American Girl, LLC

Tell it like it is

Spin a story connecting all the things you are trying to memorize. For example, if you are trying to learn the parts of a violin, you might start with the scroll and the pegs by saying that you were scrolling down the street and saw your friend Peg.

© 2008 American Girl, LLC

One step at a time

Practice one thing until you have it, and then move on.

© 2008 American Girl, LLC

All in the family

Ask your family members to join in a music jam session or play a practice game in the backyard.

© 2008 American Girl, LLC

Perk-Up-
Your-Practice
Cards

Perk-Up-
Your-Practice
Cards

Perk-Up-
Your-Practice
Cards

Perk-Up-
Your-Practice
Cards

It makes sense

Use your senses to help you memorize. Say the term out loud, write it down, read it over, and physically touch or act out what you are trying to memorize.

© 2008 American Girl, LLC

Switcheroo

Pick three key points or skills to work on. Practice one until you get it three times, and then go on to the next one. Keep switching until you have all three down.

© 2008 American Girl, LLC

In a flash

Write each term you're trying to learn, such as a symbol in music, on an index card with the definition on the back. Now put the flash cards in the car or in your backpack. Whenever you're stuck waiting, you have an instant refresher course on hand.

© 2008 American Girl, LLC

Enjoy yourself

Play, explore, and experiment with new ways of doing old things. Use your imagination and be creative. You might be surprised by the results.

© 2008 American Girl, LLC

Perk-Up-
Your-Practice
Cards

Perk-Up-
Your-Practice
Cards

Perk-Up-
Your-Practice
Cards

Perk-Up-
Your-Practice
Cards

Imitation game

Watch or listen to your favorite pro. The next time you practice, pretend you're that person.

© 2008 American Girl, LLC

Mirror, mirror

Practice your moves in front of a mirror. What do you notice? How's your posture? How's your confidence?

© 2008 American Girl, LLC

Fun with friends

Grab a friend and practice together. Take turns being the instructor and point out what the other person is doing well.

© 2008 American Girl, LLC

Look at yourself

Videotape or record yourself practicing. Make a list of five things you did well and pick one to work on. Hint: If you use the same tape each time, it's fun to track your progress!

© 2008 American Girl, LLC

Perk-Up-
Your-Practice
Cards

Perk-Up-
Your-Practice
Cards

Perk-Up-
Your-Practice
Cards

Perk-Up-
Your-Practice
Cards

A little goes a long way

Leave your equipment out and practice in five-minute intervals every few hours throughout the day.

© 2008 American Girl, LLC

Game time

Borrow a spinner (or a pair of dice) from an old board game. Use the spinner to determine the number of times you'll practice each drill.

© 2008 American Girl, LLC

Paper chase

Ask a parent or friend to help you write down skills, songs, scenes, or scales on small pieces of paper. Add some fun and silly things to do, too, and put all the papers in a jar. Whenever it's time to practice, pull out a slip of paper from the jar and complete the drill.

© 2008 American Girl, LLC

Slow and steady wins the race

Whether you are playing a song or playing a sport, rushing can lead to mistakes. Instead, go as fast as you can, not as fast as you can't. That is, go as fast as you can without making errors. Experiment with different speeds. What do you notice?

© 2008 American Girl, LLC

Perk-Up-
Your-Practice
Cards

Perk-Up-
Your-Practice
Cards

Perk-Up-
Your-Practice
Cards

Perk-Up-
Your-Practice
Cards

Code words

Use one-word acronyms to help you remember key points. For example, "S.A.F.E." might mean "Slow down," "Aim before you throw," "Focus," and "keep your Eye on the ball," or "Slow down," "Always smile at the judges," "Focus," and "Execute your piece."

© 2008 American Girl, LLC

Showtime

Put on a home talent show to practice what you know. Make invitations and tickets, too. Performing (even if it's just for your stuffed animals) counts as practice, too!

© 2008 American Girl, LLC

Make it harder

Practice blindfolded, standing on one foot, or wearing a floppy hat. Adding a new challenge to what you are doing helps you learn to stay focused and, let's face it, it's just plain fun!

© 2008 American Girl, LLC

Story time

Attach silly meanings and names to what you are doing. For example, if the song you are trying to learn reminds you of a circus, dream up a story about a circus to help you remember the verses to sing.

© 2008 American Girl, LLC